Pack Light: Thoughts for the Journey
Published by Tracee Lydia Garner

www.TeeGarner.com

© Cover Design: http://selfpubbookcovers.com/RLSather

Interior Format by

PACK *Light*

THOUGHTS FOR THE JOURNEY

Tracee Lydia Garner

January 2019
Joan,
Enjoy my story
and thank you.
Keep going
Tracee

TABLE OF CONTENTS

Also By Tracee Lydia Garner

Fiction

All That & Then Some (Family Affairs)

Come What May

The One Who Holds My Heart (sequel to Come What May)

Love Unchosen

Anchored Hearts

Deadly Affections (coming soon)
(Sequel to Anchored Hearts)

Non-Fiction

Pack Light: Thoughts for the Journey

ACKNOWLEDGEMENTS

To ALL the people who have featured in my life, even those that have caused me the most angst and prepared an atmosphere of adversity: thank you. You had your purpose and I have mine.

The staff of the Loudoun County Public Library System: there is no greater group of people (be-sides those at my place of worship or in a shoe store) than those that work for the library admin-istration. All that knowledge and helpfulness in one building... There is NO greater joy than writing this book, and seeing it produced right before my very eyes. Awesome! Everyone should try it sometime.

My family is everything. I love you SO much. #Best-DadEver (before there were #hashtags) and Jeremiah, I miss you both every day!

God. (He needs no verbiage.)

INTRODUCTION

WHAT IF ADVICE BOOKS WERE just a tad shorter? Not fiction per se (I'm sorry I can't write shorter fiction, I love it so much), but the self-help, work-family-life-type stuff? The advice, the stories, the here's-what-I-learned, now-go-do-this...

What if advice were these cute little macaroons, munched between small sips of hot tea? What if, in the span of two little (but super cute) bites, you could get petit-four-sized anecdotal advice to take with you, mull over and revisit whenever you were in the mood?

The lessons here are just that, I hope. Think of them as me preparing you to think about critical moments in your journey. Short, sweet, satisfying; just enough.

I have a disability. Before you say you don't: shh... Everyone has something, whether they want to admit it or not. Here in these pages, I want to revisit some pretty straightforward life lessons that can apply to everybody, regardless of disabled status.

The lessons I share here are not unique, but they are special in that they will give you a new perspective. Isn't that what life is? Every single day presents an opportunity to gain fresh and different ways to consider your purview. The questions that follow are required packing for the journey ahead. I like reading things that offer perspective, prompting me to "introspect" and answer pivotal questions to help me arrive at new revelations. Enjoy this time spent learning and working (OK, there *is* just a little work). Go through each of the exercises at your leisure. Then, encourage yourself and others by sharing them. That's all I ask. I can't wait to hear the stories borne from reading my lessons and revelations.

The stories (and, more importantly, the lessons) are right there in your own life, too. Take a deep breath and dig, dig just a little deeper for the nuggets and soon, like me, you'll have your own pot of hard-won gold.

Remember to pack a little light to take along with you on this journey. If it gets dark along the way, ask to sit under the light of others, so their light may reflect on you until you can harness a light of your own and let it shine for God's glory.

Take good care,

Tracee

GETTING THE MOST FROM THIS BOOK

A LITTLE BOOK OF THOUGHTS ON some of life's issues. That's my tag line for the gist of this book. Here are some things I'd like you to think about (and actually do) to allow the messages this book offers to be as impactful for you as possible as you read.

Read. Consider. Act. Evaluate. Repeat.

Try the exercises and be honest with yourself about the questions asked. No one is peeking. The only real way toward change or progress is to start with the truth.

Each day you read (and when the opportunity presents itself), try a different approach. That's what this is really about: that, just perhaps, your usual approach doesn't work, or it works partially but could use some tweaking.

Open your mind, heart, eyes and ears. In many instances - take Chapter Seven, for example, about invitations – you may think the opportunity for you to take the appropriate action just never presents itself. I caution this thought. The opportunity *is* there, but for whatever reason we often ignore it.

Challenge yourself to pray – not always for the same things and not just for the big things. We seem always to pray for large hurdles to shrink and for others to shift. Pray for the great *and* the small. Changing self is likely a greater feat than praying for other people or situations to "move on" instead. Ask for the will to bend more easily as you face adversity.

1
Queen Gimp

QUEEN GIMP

I WISH I COULD TELL YOU that "gimp" is a term I can use freely among all disability advocates alike; or perhaps that it really means Girls Improving to Make Paper, or Progress... but that is not how I use it. It's just what it is: a word I use when I am feeling some particular way about myself. My gimpiness. Eternal gimpdom. Sometimes I even give myself a pep talk that starts with, "Girl, you better Gimp It Up!"

For me, however politically incorrect it is, "gimp" is my word to say. "Hey, let's go, gimpy and all." As if to say: I have no time for that (whatever nonsense I'm experiencing) now. Keep it moving, nothing to see here – just me and my gimpiness!"

In a message I heard years ago, Dr. Joyce Meyer gently mocked people who go around lamenting: "God, why do I have to do this?", "Lord, I can't bear this – it's too hard!"; "God, *why me?*!", (You'll get her drift if you say all of this in a whiny, nasal voice.) On and on ran a string of these familiar-sounding complaints, all of which were about being somehow ill-equipped to go through trials, stress or even the shortest bout of adversity.

In the midst of this particular topic, Dr. Meyer asked a very powerful question that gave me pause – along with everyone else in TV-land, it seemed. Simply, she asked: "Why NOT you?

That short statement encourages you to ask yourself the tough question: why are *you*, of all people, such a wonderful individual that you should not have to face any adversity?

Yes, you are special – you are fearfully and wonderfully made – but the scripture did not go on to say anything about you alone being so wonderful that "thou shalt not experience difficulty," or "thou shalt have eternal beds of ease as thou maneuvers through thy time on earth."

"Why me?" I've been there and thought that, certainly. It's usually coupled with frustration, worry, fear, and/or feelings of defeat. Most often, it's triggered by opportunities where the environment is abrasive, brash or just cold. An uncomfortable atmosphere just makes whatever we're experiencing at the time seem that much worse.

The elephant in the room, of course, is that I'll never know why I had to be born with a disability. I also believe that, even if I had a reason, I doubt it'd be ultimately satisfying.

Why me?

Sometimes I ask God if I could have just a little more strength to transfer more easily: to still need help, perhaps, but to at least be able to lift myself up and over without the need for bulky equipment and human aide, plus the need to rent said expensive equipment every time I want to take a trip out of town somewhere.

When I enter a hotel, my aide rolls the Hoyer lift down the hall. Then, so the routine goes, kids and some brave adults will stare. The braver ones may even ask outright: "Momma, what's that?" It's annoying, but, at some point, I had to make peace with it. This is my life and I do the very best I can with it. And God has made it look – to others on the outside, at least – like it's *doable*.

I'm here to tell you that whatever adversity you feel incompetent to handle is, indeed, doable.

Disability and any adversity at all – up to and including the most outlandish and impossible-seeming thing you can think of – *can and will be handled*, with God's grace, by the exact person He permitted the affliction to come upon. Every day, I witness the people around me refuting the stereotypes and stigmas around disability. Yes, it is a progression toward acceptance. And please note that accepting something does not mean you like it.

What's more, you have to make peace. Those that don't make peace with whatever disease, limitation or other physical or mental barriers they face will have the hardest time coping with their day-to-day lives.

One example I encounter frequently is from those I lovingly refer to as the ADA thumpers. I have friends – even professional colleagues – that, like the bible thumpers back in the day, harp on endlessly about all manner of lack of inclusive practices, inaccessibility, non-compliance and lack of adherence to the ADA (Americans with Disabilities Act). Instead of using negotiation and reasoning to try to improve the situation, they simply complain. I have grown to realize that this approach doesn't always work. As a reformed ADA thumper myself, I continually work toward finding a balanced, gentle way to remind people of my rights and the decades-old laws which back up my right.

It is hard. I'm not arguing with that. What I am saying is that it's *much harder* when you don't learn to depend on God for daily strength, patience and corrective attitude adjustments to deal with whatever your personal issues are.

Life without God: now THAT'S hard.

I depend completely on God to assist me. With that being said, I am still human, and I will also say that the only times I'm even reminded of my limitations are in two instances:

When, like anyone, I have a really bad day. It's only because of everything *else* that went wrong on that day that I'm reminded of my set limitations. These limitations (that have been with me all along, mind you) seem especially weighty today, just because of the day's added mishaps and confrontations with others.

When I encounter attitudinal barriers. That's every day, to be frank. I may encounter a person's attitude that *places* limits on me (or that tries to, at least, which is exhausting).

The latter, let me tell you, are pretty hard to overcome. In situations where I find these barriers, I can only be present, try my best and ensure I maintain a can-do attitude. From the outside, nobody can judge your strength and your ability to solve problems creatively. And they won't ever know that you can do it, until you show them. You must not be afraid to help people understand and get past their own mental constipation. So long as you do it in love, you can't ever have regrets.

I'm very laid back. It takes a lot to make me upset, although I do get tired of fighting for something that should be happening already. I can't go around quoting laws that are not enforced and that only a small percentage of the population chooses to abide by.

One advantage I have is that my strong suit is humor. In a way that is uniquely mine, I try to bring people around to my way of thinking by reducing hostility and, in its place, try to point out areas of strife through funny things. I focus on similarities that tie us all together, rather than the small things that separate us. Do not get me wrong: I still struggle with growth in this area, but humor really does help.

How about that approach? I didn't make anyone feel bad, I didn't leave a bad taste in anyone's mouth; I simply tried a more reasonable approach, looking for a civil road toward mutually satisfying conclusions.

Truth be told, people only care about any given thing to the extent that they can get benefit out of it. Remember that whole WIIFM line: What's In It For Me? Sometimes that's a really hard line to take, because the answer is often "nothing." There's often *nothing* to be gained that's materially beneficial. Most of the gains to be had, in fact, are the warm and fuzzy things that people feel: unfortunately *not* the same things that bring additional funds to bank accounts.

What's important? It's not always popular to do the right thing, but it will cost you less grief in the long term when you do. As the time-honored saying goes: "What's right is not always popular; what's popular is not always right." And yes, when that doesn't work, permission for the gloves to come off is granted.

We all live in the same environment. In the end, all we really have going for us is the way in which we conduct ourselves. The following are a few ways you can adjust that conduct:

Make an impact on (because you can't control) the environment. The environment includes people, places and things like the weather. You can set the stage for success but you can only make an impact on what happens: you can't change it. Change occurs as a result of the impact. Be positive and be willing to flex with the bend. Remember, however, that the environment is subject to act of its own volition.

Controlling Self. This is often far more manageable than #1 – but not always. I face adversity everyday and I sometimes have to abandon original plans due to physical limitations. Yes, I may hate this. Yes, I may even be emotionally bereft (sounds better than saying I sometimes cry my eyes out) if the original plans were precious enough to me. Whatever happens, though, I will do my best to find a new approach, a new way to do something. Above all, I keep going.

Alternate Approach. Often, the same old method of approach that you usually use just doesn't work. You have to try something different. Talk with a friend who can offer alternatives. Talk with that one person who *always* has awesome ideas; someone who is not afraid to tell you the truth and, perhaps most of all, can be objective. In other words, talk to someone that doesn't have a dog in the fight.

Admitting Defeat. Often, changes occur on the advocacy front when I'm just about to give up. They also tend to occur most frequently *after* I moved on from that particular battle. This annoys me. Why?

The answer is probably that I'd been fighting for something for so long that I'm now somehow offended the result did not occur on my watch. It feels almost as if the time I spent on the issue was in vain because the change didn't happen right then.

At this point, I need to rethink and ask myself the vital question: *did change still occur*? Did people still benefit from the change? Was the outcome the same even if the method used wasn't how I would have done it? If it did change, however late I perceive it to be, *the change still happened*.

Your efforts may have had a much greater impact than you think in being a catalyst for the start of change. If you are angry that you've been saying the same thing the whole time and it didn't happen "on your watch", think about ego for just a moment. Do you feel this way simply because your ego is bruised?

Secondly, when you think back to all those times you asked for the exact thing that just happened, did it occur for someone else because they had the better approach?

If the credit is really what's important to you, that might be a problem.

If the wished-for end result did in fact occur, can you let that be enough? Was there a positive impact on someone, on a group of people or for a worthwhile cause? Shouldn't the ultimate goal be just as satisfying regardless of who the watchman happened to be when it occurred?

EXERCISE

Think of a time you wanted something (a kind of change) very strongly. What steps did you take to make it happen?

The CHANGE I desired…:

____

____

____

____

____

____

____

____

____

The IMPACT I tried to make to facilitate the change:

____

____

____

____

____

The NEW APPROACH may be to...:

If this occurred again, what will be my DIFFERENT APPROACH?:

The OBJECTIVE FRIEND/COUNSEL could be:

My DESIRED OUTCOME is to:

When will I know it's time to ADMIT DEFEAT?:

Can I truly say that EGO is not a factor here? Discuss.

____

____

____

____

____

____

____

2

Born This Way, For...

BORN THIS WAY, FOR...

AT VARIOUS POINTS IN MY life, I've often hated being called "inspiring". The label annoys me. Who wants to be inspiring?

I felt that way for a long time because I thought I could see what was behind the label – and I felt stung by the real reasons someone would use it to describe me.

I still wonder if one reason a person with a disability is often called "inspiring" is that it's a kind of code word for pity. Because... well, isn't it natural to look at others and privately count one's blessings that one is not currently in that particular situation oneself? This might be especially true of those who secretly feel that they themselves have perfect bodies and abilities.

We must be very careful about this kind of outlook on our lives. This is a type of comparison that's not good for all kinds of reasons; it's also just plain wrong. Maybe you don't use a wheelchair, but if you really think for a moment about the "lesser attributes" that you do have, you'll quickly see that we all have something.

God gave me enough grace to deal with my limitations. In my life, throughout my journey, I've come to see that

God has given me enough grace to deal with the issues, without comparing myself and my limitations to those of others.

In Chapter One, I reminded you that acceptance of a certain state does not necessarily mean you will be happy with it. Rather, it means you're acknowledging that, in a way, it's universal. Your acceptance is actually of the fact that everyone will experience a "less than" feeling at some point, no matter what cards they have been dealt.

Do you feel that you need more grace to deal with whatever it is you have? Did you seek Him and ask for it?

Change your perspective around your thoughts that tell you, *"Well, I got my own problems, but I ain't got* those *problems."* That sort of comparative thinking is not a great way to get through the day, yet that statement is one that so many of us make from time to time.

I find many other people with disabilities encouraging and inspiring – but not because their disability is "better" than mine. Do you see how awful that sounds? Disability is a type of condition. There is no hierarchical structure on the Ladder of Disability, and there should never be any.

The inspiration I feel should come from a place that says I'm still okay, no matter what. I'm still enough, in spite of whatever baggage that makes you compare yourself to other human beings and come away feeling better or less than. You have to recognize that while you feel one way today, it can all change in the blink of an eye. It's very important to take no moment for granted.

Lastly, I hated being considered inspiring because I didn't want to have to motivate people. What's wrong with motivating people, you ask? Well, one of my problems with it is that our world has taken life coaching to a whole new level. Even I need to be motivated from time to time, upbeat as I normally am, and for this I look to my small group of encouragers. These are the people that buoy me up when I feel down. They don't look at me incredulously, or ask me, "Oh my god – again!" In any area, we need support, help and encouragement to keep living our life to the fullest and to stay in the race until the very end.

I consider it a blessing to do what I can to encourage, but that view took time – and notice I said "encourage". I often prefer this word over "motivate".

Finally, do not mistake a little encouragement for taking your hand and all-out *dragging* you to the finish line. This is not what I'm speaking of. Over the years, I have had to let certain people go. These are the people who take and take and take, never seeming to offer anything in return. You know who they are. They only show up to unload problems, get a word of encouragement and be showered with a plethora of reasons why they are so wonderful. Then they suddenly have to leave. They don't usually have time to return the favor of lending an ear.

While I urge you to be an *encourager*, I'm not talking about being an *enabler* for those who fit the above description. Over the course of your journey, you will always need to ensure that you have a way to maneuver yourself away from such people, avoiding giving of your time and protecting your personal energy from their harmful influence.

When I speak to a group of people in my work, help others work on their problems and reach their goals in life, deliver a speech or workshop or just "show up" in life, period, I receive the eventual validation that I'm making progress. Being "inspiring" really isn't enough but it is the impetus for change. It all has to start somewhere. On days when I feel so very tired and "inspired out" – it's then that it's the most important for me to return to my purpose and to and to narrow the lens on the wonderful opportunity I have to encourage others.

EXERCISE

Let's examine your thoughts here, below.
What or who inspires *you*?

I am inspired by:

Why?

List some things you feel you could never have. (It could be getting to a different level at work, for example, or simply attaining a particular feeling.)

Why do these things seem impossible?

Who, in or out of your circle, is doing that supposedly-impossible thing?
(potential mentor?/even if not directly, how else could you study them up close?)

How do you believe they are able to do this?
(list three things you observe about them)

What do you commit to learning to be better at?
(list limitations and action items for each) [expand on definition of "action item"]

Limitation # 1: ______________________

Action Item/s: ______________________________

____

____

____

____

____

Limitation # 2: ______________________________

____

____

____

____

____

Action Item/s: ______________________________

____

____

____

____

____

Limitation # 3: ______________________________

____

____

____

____

____

Action Item/s: ______________________________

____

____

____

____

____

3

Alter, But Don't Let It Go

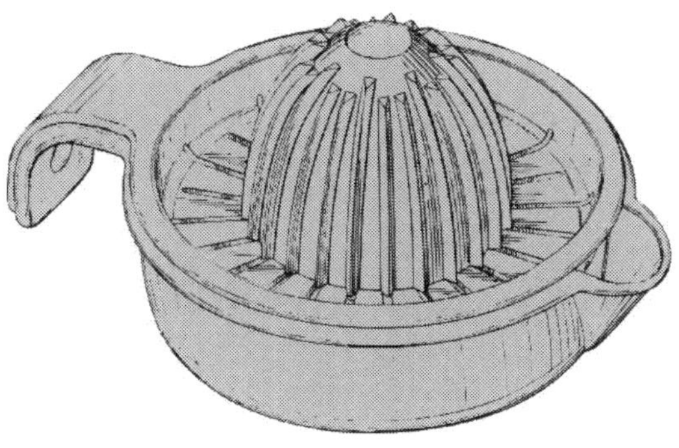

ALTER, BUT DON'T LET IT GO

I KNOW, I KNOW: THE FICTIONAL Queen Elsa of Arendelle in Walt Disney's Frozen told you to Let It Go… but now I'm here to tell you that the best-selling animated film of all time has it just a teeny little bit wrong.

"Let it go" is great advice regarding the things of old that you've been holding onto for too long. However, this isn't a mantra that is applicable to everything. Letting It Go should never be the blanket option for life's "didn't work outs". Certainly, there are things we're holding on to for much too long. These things can manifest themselves, for example, as years-long relationships that never approach the idea of getting married. These things could be the habits forever separate from the thought of improving. These things are even beliefs so tightly held that they reject any thought of being made aware.

Do you see what I'm saying? The idea is that whatever you're holding on to shouldn't always be "let go". It all depends on what it is. The second question is: could the thing you're clinging onto be better kept in some "altered" way?

Due to my physical limitations, I've often had no choice but alter to my dreams. I could spend my life, as I have seen some do, searching, hoping and praying for a cure for the neuromuscular issues that make my life more difficult. Things are doable, certainly, but difficulty remains in some facets of living this life. Don't get me wrong: if a cure were to come – and I believe that one day it will – I'll certainly be very happy; but the chances of it coming anytime soon, multiplied by the likelihood of that particular strand matching the infinitesimal number of types of issues, is improbable at best. Please know that it's not that I don't believe it can come: my awareness that there are so many false hopes, partials and studies gone awry simply means that I will embrace that exciting time *when it arrives*.

In the meantime, I, along with many other people with disabilities, maintain that disability is a part of life. In general, I find that my time is better spent getting on with this life and making a difference however I possibly can. If you subscribe to the belief that God's grace is sufficient, you are not concerned about cures. You believe His grace *is* sufficient: enough to deal with and even shine in the face of adversity.

My early dream of becoming one of Janet Jackson's back-up dancers just wasn't going to be coming true. While I still believe that you should never, ever give up on your dreams, I let go of that particular one and moved on to others.

Another let-go dream of mine is that of living on my own and having my own house. Many years ago, I visited condos, and apartment complexes, looked at square footage. I had my lists: my wishes, my deal breakers and my ideal amenities for the complex where I would live. I saw some beauties and some duds. I knew exactly what I wanted.

One time, while I was out shopping and doing my normal thing, I even bought these pretty, red-and-silver salt and pepper shakers for the new house… that I didn't yet own. I told myself I would just put them away for a time and have them ready to go… you know, later, when the dream eventually unfolded.

Time moved on and the issues around my disability grew worse. At twenty-something years of age, I was still living with my parents. This continues to be an awesome experience, but at one time, I wanted out. I so wanted my own space, wanted to live my life solo for a while. Honestly, I got the most caught up in the decorating: the idea of putting together my own space, buying dinner plates and chargers and "setting up house". As I grew up and matured, I began to realize that the dream had been highly glamorized.

When my father passed away, the only thing I could think about was the loneliness that I would feel in a place of my own – not to mention the help that I needed, plus so many more issues around safety and home maintenance that would be required if I obtained the dream. Gradually, that dream began to lose its luster. I knew I wasn't likely to save what I needed and to do my due diligence. If this was really what I said I wanted, there would be an overwhelming amount of change and work.

I wasn't putting in place what I needed to do and I wasn't inclined to sacrifice the things that would have to go in order to get there. Without those key moves, how, then, could the dream be obtained? When the housing market busted, my feelings were along the lines of: "Oh yay! Here's permission (or a cop out really) to not look toward that dream as something I desire." Moreover, as I tell my Mother to this day, moving wasn't about not being with her: it was a healthy feeling that I needed to have had as a growing adult. I know that many parents likely wish their millennial felt as I did back then, but many are content to stay put. I honestly believe that's okay. There's a difference between paying a little rent to support oneself while living at home and being a bit of a freeloader who has to be reminded to do things like take the trash out. The latter wasn't me. The issues around my desire to own a home and move out centered more upon feelings that my independence was wrapped up in my living status.

This chapter sounds like it's about defining a level of success that feels right to you. You can glean that here too, perhaps; but it's really more about accepting that, whatever your situation is, the dream just may require a different lens. I still have places in my shared home that are all mine, and the things that excited me about the original dream are things I still have control over. I have places that are like my little living room, my room, plus other living spaces throughout the house.

I have to make peace with the fact that a roommate of some sort, whether related to me or not, is essential for my peace of mind and safety. I have to embrace the positives of that situation, and fortunately those are plentiful. I came to realize that, with my physical issues, care and maintenance of an actual house wouldn't have been what I thought it might be. Lastly, I have to embrace the concept that, depending on the outlook I choose, there are still small but satisfying ways to make my dream come (sort of) true. The problem centers on the illusion that your independence (or *insert your issue here*) is controlled solely by you.

One of the ways I make my dream come true is through my books. In my fictional tales, I create a sense of space and an imagined living environment each and every day – and that's fun. I still orchestrate my own life. I'm still in charge. *You* are in charge of altering the dream to suit your abilities. Your task is to think up ways to reach the dream's end somehow. Above all, never abandon it entirely.

While the ultimate design of any of your dreams may not be what you originally had in mind, your choice lies in what your heart and mind decide to make of it.

EXERCISE

Spend some time thinking about the original dream. Write about your dream and yourself in the space below. Pretend you're sitting outside on a bright clear day: you can't believe you've arrived at your dream! Write about your feelings and then list the things you see out in front of you that perhaps you cannot believe you have obtained.

Now, at the present time, what are the things that are currently blocking this view for you?

Be honest and ask yourself if the dream is tied to some kind of status or a symbol of power.

Why isn't it tied to power or status?

If the dream must be altered to be at all realistic, how does it change?

Is this alteration still satisfying?

Why, or why not?

One important step is to carefully and thoroughly evaluate the initial goal: the core of your dream. Is it in need of altering? Might it still be doable in a different way? You'll need to figure that out. Seek God and ask for clarity.

If you will alter your dream, it's a process that must be revisited, as with all other dreams and goals you hold dear for your life. If the new version of the dream is to be realized, what steps will you take toward it? How will you make it happen?

In Chapter Five, you'll learn how to develop and uncover the Network you'll need to support you and help to foster this part of your journey.

4

DO OVER?

DO OVER?

I CAN'T HELP BUT THINK ABOUT the reasons one of my favorite pop stars in the entire world (and many a deceased famous musician before him) could not have a happy life-ending.

In their prime, that best-selling album or sold-out concert was the gauge of their happiness. They seemed to try really hard every single night on stage to capture a repeat performance of the same feelings that they originally sang about and presumably felt… only to become exhausted, worn out and dissatisfied because it didn't quite play out like that very first time when things were just perfect. They spent so much time trying (and failing) to recreate that same euphoric feeling over and over again.

It's no way to live.

I think back to the time when I won the First Time Writer's Contest at the tender age of 23. The process of birthing my book – the award that changed my life – a trip to NYC – a monetary advance – AND publication of my very first story. These were all such wonderful things.

As much as I'd like to be 23 again, things sadly just aren't going to happen like that ever again.

This was a time in my life of which I'll cherish the memory forever: one that I even reminisce on from time to time. The thing is, I'm reliving it only in my mind, and only occasionally. It's not something that I spend eons of my time trying to recreate. That's just not possible. Certain factors (like the age of 23, for one) cannot be attained ever again. Ultimately, as fun as that time was, there is still so much joy and happiness and so many gleeful moments to be had in the right-now.

We die a little inside when we lose the ability to move on.

What can't you let go of? Why can't you? Would you say you're really living your life – or are you just existing from one moment to the next, all the while hoping for a return of that stomach fluttering high you had long ago?

Are you looking for some way that you can get a repeat performance? That's not a good thing. The only actual replays in life occur on television and using your DVR.

Here and now, you don't have do-overs. What you do have, however, are new mercies and opportunities that are as real and present as the excitement waiting to be uncovered.

I think it's unfortunate that we consider New Year's Day our lone annual opportunity to think of resolutions and goals to do things right. Planning for and plotting the year ahead IS extremely important: a very validating exercise that I do myself. This sort of collective review of everything should not be discounted – *but what if we could have that every day?* The year is such a large chunk of space and studies show that by March we've fizzled out on all those resolutions we spent time creating with the best of intentions. How come we have no real problem with abandoning those the minute they don't work out as we'd hoped?

Such grand ideas are almost too large, too mammoth to tackle. So what could you do? Take a more daily or weekly approach? You could consider what it was that excited you about that past accomplishment. Every day, how could you look for a small nugget of victory amid your search for those same mountain-high feelings?

If you really think about it, you'll even start to feel thankful that that single event *can't* be recreated. Otherwise, what would you have to look forward to? How much fun would it be to keep reliving the same moment over and over again? Take the early '90's film *Groundhog Day*. Those recurring events get really old – until Bill Murray's character finally understands what he needs to do to get it right and move on with his life. (Certainly, by Hollywood's logic, if Bill had continued to enjoy repeat performances, the movie would most likely have been about how great it is to experience the same thing over and over again!) Who wants to watch a movie like that? And, dare I ask, when would it ever end?

Every single day presents that same opportunity: to wipe the slate clean, and carry with you only the great things you learned from your past. You have the option to try again, and to apply that learning to the days following. Whatever you *feel* you didn't get exactly right the first time is up for second takes. I say whatever you feel you didn't get right because, after all, we always think of ourselves as messing up. But some things, in hindsight, worked out perfectly in any case. You have to trust that whatever positive things happened in the past were indeed great at that time, *but* today presents an opportunity to do that much more.

EXERCISE

This Magic Moment

Briefly, take a few moments to describe an awesome time in your life. Write about what's happening, paint a picture of the day/time/place: where are you? Pretend you are telling a friend who wasn't there but desperately wanted to share in the joyous occasion with you. If you believe that you haven't yet experienced such a special moment, I would argue that you have! You've just dressed it down as insignificant – not big enough, according to you, to warrant talking about. If you are stuck at feeling the latter, tell the story and talk about the moment when you imagine that you WILL have that time in your life.

Why was/is this time so special?

What would you wish you had done if you knew you would be leaving the earth tomorrow?

Did you find ways to speed up trying to make the moment happen? Did you let the moment go and figure out a different way?

How can you create the happy moments described above *now*? What's holding you back?
What's stopping you?

Are these valid limitations? Are these simply things you've made up to make you feel better about not pursuing your goals with abandon?

Let's say that one thing that you desire is right here. Right beside you. Right in this room. What is it? In this scenario, what would you do first, second, third and so on? Who would be there? Who would not be there? Why?

____

____

____

____

____

____

____

____

____

____

How would you feel after the moment has passed?

____

____

____

____

____

____

____

____

____

____

5

THE NETWORK

THE NETWORK

ALL OF US NEED A network, whether we believe it or not. We as individuals need other people in our life to make things work. It's just part of the human genome. Living organisms require various elements to survive – including other humans, as part of what's often called a network.

Take time to build your network. You can think of your network as a toolkit. Every item in the kit solves a different problem. Whatever the overarching issue is that you're dealing with, you'll need a diverse network to tackle complex issues and to provide the necessary support. Plus, you will need to start counting yourself as part of other people's networks: being part of the team that's on hand to help them through the life issues they will also face.

The most important aspect of the network is to ensure that others are shining in their specific gifts. If you've never taken a spiritual gifts class, you will want to find a local class and sign up right away. Any such time spent discovering more about yourself and your best attributes can only help you. You'll start to offer your time in pursuit of things that are more in line with what you CAN do. Knowing self can ensure you don't become exhausted and burnt out simply because you're in the wrong position within the network. *Doing what you were not designed to do only promotes frustration, burn out, fatigue and grumpiness.*

Never go with what you *think* your gifts are. Do try to take the right assessment to get an accurate picture. Here is a list of spiritual gifts:

Administration
Knowledge
Apostleship
Leadership
Discernment
Mercy
Evangelism
Miracles
Exhortation
Pastor/Shepherd
Faith
Prophecy
Giving
Serving/Ministering
Healing
Teaching
Interpretation of Tongues
Tongues
Wisdom

What did you find in that gift list that spoke to you as an individual? What are your gifts?

Personally, I love teaching. Since I was twenty-five, I have taught continuing-education classes in writing, publishing and small-business marketing/promotion at the local community college. I didn't even know I would enjoy it as much as I do.

I also don't mind paperwork. Most people hate paperwork: they can't make sense of it, they can't seem to get organized and they can often become immobilized by distraction from the convoluted questions that are asked therein. In my line of social work, if you want any kind of benefit, you will need to complete some kind of paper form to qualify for it. These benefits often offer lifesaving monetary support. In short, paperwork is par for the course if you want something. So I guess you could say I also have a gift for administration. Not the most glamorous gift, perhaps, but there you go.

Finally, I have the gift of helps or *encouragement* and/or *helps*. Helps falls under administration by the way. If we go back to that whole thing around "inspiring" back in chapter two, sometimes you are unaware that you're even doing it and I would rather it be around the fact that I simply am demonstrative of a can do attitude and that often "helps," a lot.

No matter how hard you work on building it up, your network won't always provide every single kind of support there is for any given situation under the sun. It will be important to strategize with the rest of network and think objectively. Ultimately, if you don't end up finding a person to fill every gap and meet each one of your support needs, it's not the end of the world.

I will say this: in the relational department, I have found that the practice of building and maintaining quality relationships is one of the most difficult parts of life. Over time, you will put lots of effort into various relationship-building components, yet still not always get to see the results of your time and energy bearing fruit.

Pastor T. D. Jakes, a best-selling author and evangelist from one of the largest mega-churches in Texas, observes in his book *He-Motions* that "*those of us who exhibit audacious strength will also be the ones that no one feels the need to encourage.*" Per his title, Jakes talks about this being exhibited and felt most strongly in men. I would argue, though, that many groups of women experience the same exact thing. Bottling up emotions, carrying lots of different weights, multi-tasking between running the family unit, their work, their "side hustle"/other work, their community, their volunteerism…

Doing all these things makes it seem from the outside as if many women can do it all without fail and without the need for supporters or network participants. When you're doing so well, who could possibly think you need any assistance? Is it any wonder you don't get any, when you look pretty competent to others looking on in awe? They have no idea what you go through to make it all happen. People are unaware of the sacrifices, the internal struggle and the private loneliness felt as you struggle to appear as if all is well, or at least that all is calm and completely under control.

I remember a time when I asked someone for help in organizing an important church function. I was planning a large gathering where I needed to sell tickets, evaluate and decide on an appropriate and cost-effective venue, work with a guest speaker, find the right entertainment or musical guest *and* come up with a budget. On top of all that, I needed to work with other area churches to market the event and pull it all together.

I sought out the head of a similar ministry. From what I'd seen, as well as what I'd heard from others, I knew that this person's event creations were always beautiful. People had a joyous time and she had great, sold-out attendance. I wanted to do it like she did. Also, as I was pretty new, I thought she might help me navigate the many options for an event theme.

I didn't perceive myself an awesome event planner back then – although I love it now – and the creativity she exhibited in her event planning attracted me. I thought we might share ideas: collaborate. Maybe, I daydreamed, we would even work together on a joint venture some day, combining our ministries for even greater success. I was excited to hear what she would share with me.

Needless to say, my glowing visions of how our encounter would go – her gleeful acceptance and desire to help me as I had asked – just did not happen as I had imagined. Quite simply, she didn't help me when I asked. She didn't help me at all. My requests hit a brick wall. Despite being referred to her by many who said her events were spectacular, I had to conclude from her response that our working together wasn't to be.

A polite decline would have been fine with me. Of course people are busy: we're all overwrought with activity and we give away a great deal of our time in an effort to help others. However, her precise choice of words pierced to my heart and made me feel quite alone:

"She seems very creative. She will figure it out."

(By the way, one of the strangest aspects was that I was sitting right there and she spoke of me in the third person.)

Yes, perhaps I am "creative", but I hadn't done what she was doing. I didn't know the protocols of requesting this or that, or working with hospitality to get the right amount food, beverages and paper products. I had no idea how to put in a request to get the off-site venue paid.

Drum roll: when push came to shove, my event worked out fine, although it would have been nice to have a guide for my initial, fumbling and hesitant steps.

Here's a thought: *you can work it out.* It won't be perfect and you may have a few bumps and scrapes along the way, but don't let that deter you from moving forward. God will always be there for you – always. But, while you're going through whatever it is, you don't *know* you can work it out. You will have times where you feel snubbed. Why didn't that person help me? Why do they help everyone else but me?

Many may argue that I really didn't need help. That's fine. Dorothy didn't need the Wizard, remember? What she *did* need was the support network that accompanied her along the journey to figure that out. (Many literary critics, and some layperson-realists, say that Dorothy's friends along the way were figments of her imagination – perhaps even archetypes of her actual family… but that's a whole different book.)

Point is, anyone could say they didn't need something after the fact. But would you have said that if my event had failed? If Dorothy withered and had a nervous breakdown… well, that would have been a terribly depressing trajectory for a children's story to take, in any case.

No matter how competent we perceive people to be, everyone will need someone to offer a kind word of encouragement. Why do we perceive the successful ones to be in such little need of help?

I'm sure that when we start looking, there is more help out there than we can actually stand. Likewise, it's perfectly fine, even laudable, to admit when you yourself can be of no assistance. If you are not the one to help, though, can you offer an alternative? Can you assist the requestor in other ways, maybe by identifying someone whose knowledge base reflects the subject matter they seek help about?

If you are not the person to help, what prevents you from recommending an alternative (I call this resource referral)? In your willingness to provide such resource referral, you have fulfilled a double purpose: you haven't left the person without a possible alternative, and you have also acknowledged the need for assistance even when the assistance could not be enacted by you, directly.

Finally, if the person in question is coming to you presenting a recurring need, perhaps they need other systems in place to help mitigate these recurring incidents. Remember not to let others' seemingly insurmountable challenges become a burden on you. Can you strategize to help this person identify other helpful systems? Can you offer to help them create a list of workable solutions that will get them closer to their desired end goal? Can you point them in the right direction, even if it's not an outright fix?

I'm not advising you to help people to the point of exhaustion. Know your own limitations. *You can't help everyone, nor should you try.*

Often, you'll find that you know some other capable person who may be able to help. Note: this does *not* translate as volunteering that other person for the job without their consent. Rather, this is telling the person who is struggling that you may have someone in mind who could help them, but that you'll need to check with that individual first and get back to the requestor.

Even as I write this, I know that some person will look at this chapter and think I'm making too big a deal out of my (or anyone's) simple inability to be more self-sufficient. I would argue that the network you need has most likely been present all along. You just choose to reduce its members to "friends" status. And they *are* friends: that's fine, but consider each one in turn more carefully. Think on the different things they offer at different times in your life. YOU are also part of a network, offering different solutions to life's common issues, often already shining in your best gift to that particular friend or loved one who needs you.

Asking for help shows humility. It demonstrates your awareness that you *don't* have it all figured out, and that's good. We all need HELP!

Finally, we have to be careful of jealousy. I don't know that jealousy was the motivating factor in my earlier event-planning example, exactly; but as I grow in my knowledge, this seems more and more plausible. At twenty and even thirty years of age, however, that suggestion seemed truly incomprehensible, petty and quite silly. Really? Me – jealous? Why would you say that?

I felt like I needed the help with the project I described, and I wanted to get some assistance. Hence the Big Ask. The more we're shunned sometimes, the more we do one of two things in response. We either get angry enough to work it out independently to the point of exhaustion, trying to prove something to ourselves and others – but at what expense? – Or, at the other extreme, we feel defeated, go off somewhere and do something drastic.

Sadly, many people without the right network of support around them do the most devastating things. Tragically, the most extreme cases end in suicide. Many more cause harm to themselves or others. I'm not suggesting that one "no" response inevitably leads to this kind of destruction, but what if it happens repeatedly?

We may ask others for assistance and we should. But after a shutdown or two, it's hard to keep asking.

It wasn't at all about needing help. We have to say to ourselves that we are going to be the type of person to come alongside someone and assist them, lift them up, encourage and support them where we can. We'd want no less in this life for ourselves.

EXERCISE

List people in your current network: who they are and what they provide:

Below is a sample "base network" to get you started, but there could be more (or fewer) people involved in yours. Remember that some roles in your network will overlap: that is, one person can fulfill more than one role in the same network. Examine your network closely and see what you come up with.

CHEERLEADER / ENCOURAGER.

This is usually a close friend or parent/person who raised you.

Who:

____

____

____

____

Are they a good fit for this role?

____

____

____

____

Why or why not?

____

____

____

____

REALIST.

This is the person who is painfully honest with you – but you want that (even when you don't want to admit it and often dislike hearing what they say.)

Who:

____

____

____

____

Are they a good fit for this role?

____

____

____

____

Why or why not?

____

____

____

____

SOUNDING BOARD / CLOSE FRIEND (OR SPOUSE).

Sharing problems will often feel safest with this person. You may have an intimate relationship with them and you should feel that you can exhibit your vulnerability without harm or harsh criticism. Note that when problems are complex and not necessarily standard-issue (i.e. not the sort of "general-life" issues that pretty much everyone has experienced), it will be vitally important to be fair to this person. You'll need to respect their boundaries and thus remember when to seek professional advice. Try to be aware that your problems may be much deeper and more complex than even your Sounding Board can handle. Talking to a professional can help you to gauge the complexity of your issue and to establish whether you will require ongoing professional support.

Who:

____
____
____
____

Are they a good fit for this role?

____
____
____
____

Why or why not?

____
____
____
____

LOGISTICIAN.

This person may have skills in digging deeper and helping you get organized to tackle a specific project in your life.

Who:

____

____

____

____

Are they a good fit for this role?

____

____

____

____

Why or why not?

____

____

____

____

RESOURCE SPECIALIST.

This could well be the same person as the Logistician. This person knows where to get anything and everything you could possibly need. You can ask them almost anything and, though they might not have it themselves, they know where to get it.

Who:

____

____

____

____

Are they a good fit for this role?

____

____

____

____

Why or why not? __________________________

____

____

____

Think about who you are in the list above. I am the:

____

____

____

____

How do you feel about being this person?

____

____

____

____

Do you wish you fulfilled some other role? Yes / No
What role and why?

____

____

____

____

____

Now, who are you missing?

Remember that people also come into your life for a season. You may find that the people who are in your network today may later move on, having fulfilled their purpose in your life – and this is okay.

Let's examine whom you may be missing. I'm missing the following types of people from my network:

Who:

Why / what can they add?

Who:

Why / what can they add?

Who:

Why / what can they add?

6

Fight the Bullies

FIGHT THE BULLIES

OUR PURPOSE IN ACCEPTING A challenge is for the betterment of others.

Notice that the title of this chapter does not say to fight *YOUR* bullies. It says fight *the* bullies. Also note this chapter is a little longer as it examines a little deeper, some complexities in the set up.

When my long-time boss passed away suddenly a few years ago, I had no idea his death would start a major downward spiral for me in the workplace. I also did not know that I would inherit another "boss" as I moved forward in my career.

While I always knew in my head that life went on regardless of grief, loss and death, this was a major adjustment. My boss's replacement came to me in the form of a supervisor who worked mainly at the parent office. This person had been in the position for just two years. I'd been there almost eight.

It was hard. My former boss and I had really worked to develop the center where I would now continue to work solo on the issues for our entire region.

My old boss, I felt was a true manager and had a way

with people. It had been so much fun working for and with him. He was fair and encouraging, and he trusted me because I was doing a good job. I really loved my job and I felt my passion showed.

The new boss I inherited, who for brevity's sake I'll call NB, didn't know anything about me. As it turned out, I wasn't above proving myself. With my disability, I was used to trying to prove myself, attempting to compensate for the occasional "less-than" thoughts I experienced.

I learned that sometimes you just don't get the opportunity to grieve before someone is asking you to do something else – and to get it done *now*. When the person above you is under pressure, that pressure is passed on to you. You need to make time for the grieving process, or else the pressure of the day-to-day – the other person's inability to understand, plus the fact that they have no clue what's going on and moreover, they don't care. This will wear you down.

What's more, prior to my old boss passing away, one of my other colleagues in another office had decided he couldn't take NB (his former supervisor) any more. I would be called in to take my departing colleague's entire caseload, and the general pressure would mount. Driving an hour each way to the main office when my own office was only ten minutes away was tiring. To complicate matters further, I needed to have surgery and my health was steadily declining.

The battle started when performance review time came. I received my first poor performance rating.

It seemed to come out of nowhere. I had had only one poor performance rating ever in the past. The review also did not take place at the scheduled time. The fact that I had worked for NB for such a short time only compounded my surprise at having the discussion so soon. I got a Performance Improvement Plan and the experience put me on notice that this was real and that I had better start viewing what was happening a little more seriously.

I expressed my concern to NB's superior, but they appeared to be on NB's side and were themselves eventually terminated just months later. That left only NB and myself, plus an interim director, alone together.

With NB's ally out of the picture, I thought the situation might settle somewhat. Conversely, it was almost as if the introduction of an "interim" person made them even more aloof, doing only the basics of the essential work and forgetting interpersonal relationships entirely. The interim largely over looked the havoc being wreaked on the employees. After all, the work was getting done, even as NB's small team (with myself included) limped along growing increasingly disgruntled.

I refused to sign my PIP. After all it's an agreement that seems to be a catalyst toward a long dark road with firing as the end result. I couldn't take it any more. The behavior that I felt constituted harassment didn't improve, and I was not about to sit around and wait to be fired. I didn't see it ending without somebody sounding the alarm.

Writing had saved me in other facets of my life – it was the thing I reached for the most often when I needed help. I wrote out what I had to say and illustrated the grievances. I even sat on it for a time, considering, praying and deciding what ultimately to do with it. I even let a neutral party review it. Soon, I sent it to the president of the Board of Directors. Following this, we had a meeting.

While I was told I had valid concerns, I was also told that:

I had made serious accusations, and

I had circumvented "the process." I hadn't really. Before writing the letter, I had informed the supervisor that I felt I was being unfairly targeted and expressed concern. Nothing changed. A letter (and thus a paper trail) seemed to me the next logical course of action.

My letter was eventually shared with NB and, while there was some nominal effort to cease and desist the behavior, there was still an underlying tone of hostility toward me. In front of others, however, the atmosphere was cordial.

I felt alone. I knew others that had gone through what I was experiencing now, which somehow made it all the harder to take lying down. Three employees before me had thrown in the towel and, rather than duel with this difficult person, they had resigned. I was particularly annoyed with the last person to leave, who left a trail of incomplete work, a large caseload, and a real mess for me to straighten out. I was hurt. I wish I could have encouraged that last person, even if he still left, to document what was happening. Then, if nothing more, there would at least have been some kind of pattern established.

Why, I wondered, was it so hard for people to stand up to NB?

Perhaps I loved my job more than they did; perhaps people really aren't as strong as you'd hope they'd be; perhaps they too felt so alone that it was easier to bow out than to stay and fight. (Sadly, we often choose our battles this way.)

It's likely a combination of all those reasons.

While my own battle was temporarily on hold, others soon grew tired of NB as well, of course they would, NB was finding additional victims. When another new head honcho came in, I was finally moved from being supervised by NB. Instead. The head honcho was in charge.

I was happy for a time, but was also saddened to learn that NB had printed out and stacked the deck against me, pre-loading my new-new boss with reports, e-mails and other correspondence. I felt like I didn't get a clean slate, to say the least. Every time NB and I met to discuss whatever, I should have realized their note taking wasn't to recall action steps for themselves later on. I wasn't paying attention in the early stages.

I was relieved that NB was no longer my supervisor, but I was still disappointed that three others before me had opted to leave their job – and the fourth casualty caused me the most sadness because I realize that perhaps they felt they were too tired, too old and perhaps not savvy enough to keep up with the load of negativity being so officiously documented about them.

I enjoyed and valued my job, so you could say my letter was a manifesto of sorts. I wasn't going out with out a fight and realizing the consequences I felt really about trying the course least popular. If you push back even a little, at least you sound the alarm. You show you're not going to take this lying down. If you're wrong, then the end is likely near; but at least you can hold your head up when you say you tried.

Later, after others had been on the receiving end of the treatment I had already experienced, many of them were quick to complain to me, stating that they had been unaware of what I'd been going through before (even though I did express some concern). Surprise: *It was only relevant now that they too were experiencing it.* I had just conducted myself in the same, exact manner.

I will take this time to affirm that, in a work setting, it can be very difficult to find support. When your own ship is sailing with relative ease, the act of reaching out and trying to help another sailor whose boat is in trouble could pull you under. Why would you risk it? You have a lot to lose.

Later, I would learn at a staff meeting (I was calling in via conference and not present) that NB had resigned. Although I was surprised, I felt no *schaudenfreude* (joy at another's loss). I had already achieved my own goal, which was simply to escape from NB as my supervisor. The only sadness I felt stemmed from the knowledge that those four people who left before me could have made a change. Had they written a simple letter, or accessed the proper channels to complain, or made any sort of notes about the ways in which they had been treated unfairly – then at least, when it was my turn, the index of previous experiences would already be there as a source of support and even encouragement. I cringe when I think about how many other people might have been terminated and when would an upper level manager be aware of what was happening.

I wasn't ready to leave. I liked what I did and I believe the others who had already left did too. The difference was that I, unlike them, wasn't ready to bow out. I had to fight. Perhaps those before me had another job lined up; perhaps they were just ready to leave at that time. I don't know about all of them, I only know about the one who retired just before NB left. Each time we speak, as I update him on what's happening at his former workplace, there is a sense of underlying regret: a constant unspoken lament, with the growing realization that perhaps he should have tried a little harder; that just a little push back may have meant that he was still gainfully employed today.

When I was fighting back, there was no guarantee that I would still be gainfully employed at the end. Between the risks inherent in documenting the bullying incidents and being beholden to others' responses to my letter, I might easily have lost the battle and been fired too. But even if that happened, I constantly remind myself that I would still be proud of having done *something*. Doing nothing is what causes my colleague the most grief to this day. He's still out of a job, but he did nothing and that's the difficult piece to swallow. He has and he will need to move on.

The other thing about taking on a bully is that you need to keep your eyes open to what others are going through. Not only did I work in a remote office, I'm never was a gossip hound. I found out information late and often found myself wondering when did that happen? In my professional setting I was what you call "Johnny come lately" to the news of the day. But I didn't mind that label. Secondly and more importantly, when my friend complained to me about the issues they were experiencing, was I really listening? Did I truly understand that their end was near, or did I merely placate them with empty responses like, "Oh, it's alright," or "You'll be okay" or even passive suggestions like "choose your battles"? This was a battle worth taking on.

I'll hope not to repeat the mistake of underestimating the significance of what another person is telling me. In future, I hope to spend some more time with whoever has confided in me, work out the issues and help them strategize a path toward a desirable end result.

I took on the bully because the end result mattered to me. To my detriment, though, I only took on the bully after she became MY bully. I learned that *you have to take on the bully whether they're "yours" or not* – because the end result matters not only to you, but to those before and after you. Make their way easier if you can.

What if everyone acted and conducted themselves in a way that says "whatever affects you, affects me," instead of pretending that the person being bullied in the corner is having an awesome time.

The bell is ringing. To succeed in this life, you'll need your boxing gloves.

EXERCISE

Have you ever tried to ignore a bully only to see them grow larger?

List examples of any bullies in your life. How do you (or did you) fight against them?

Under which circumstances might you "throw in the towel" against someone who was bullying you?

(Among other potential benefits, the answer to this question may help you in recognizing a losing battle and giving yourself permission to move on.)

What (or who) could help you fight a bully?

If you do NOT fight the bully, what is at stake?

____
____
____
____
____
____
____
____
____
____

If the bully wins, what will you do?

____
____
____
____
____
____
____
____
____
____

What positives can you glean from the experience?

____
____
____
____
____

Is what the bully suggest really not the case or are you unwilling to admit any part in the situation?

Are there any steps you can take or even workshops you might seek to learn to deal and communicate better?

7

THE INVITATION

THE INVITATION

WELL, I TOLD YOU AT the start that this book was just some of my thoughts: anecdotes for the journey. We've come to the end, arriving at my final chapter and lesson.

I'll now take the delicious liberty of quoting myself. I have a particular line that I use often: for example, when I was selected as a "40 Under 40" award recipient in 2013. I was selected, along with thirty-nine other individuals under 40 years of age, to be recognized for contributions in business and community. In an interview for that event, I made a statement that I try to bring up whenever someone asks me to share something significant to me. It's really my mantra for life. Simply:

If you're at the table and you look around and everyone sitting there looks just like you, you should find an exit.

What could possibly be achieved in a room where everyone wears the same thing, everyone shops at the same place and everyone's brain-functions produce the same views?

What is also important is the *"why" factor* behind people's refusal to change, invite change and push for change. I get it: there is a certain amount of comfort in the "norm".

Asking for change is easy for me, you might say. I can easily find things to gripe about when I'm a woman with a disability who is also black. Can't do much about that. I will say, though, that when you introduce different perspectives – when more people are at the table – you can solve complex problems. You can move mountains. The problem with sameness is that you'll likely come up with similar solutions (that probably also won't work). What's worse is that, inevitably, you'll always omit a group of people. In business (not that that's my area of expertise) it seems that the goal is to market your product to as many people as you believe will consume it. You can't do that with a brand that speaks to only one person. When money is involved, imagine the bottom line increase when you first change the images and the word choice to reflect diversity. Now I may be talking someone's language.

Many times, I've been in a meeting or at a networking event where someone is clearly selling something to everyone but me. When this happens, I'll often just go online or to another company where I feel more welcomed and buy the same thing. Whenever I can, I let the person know that they are missing a business opportunity by failing to include me. I work, I have disposable income, and I would likely have bought what you have to sell. I was here, the timing was right, you and I were present: let's overlook prejudice and make that transaction already!

I would clarify my quote by reminding you that you shouldn't ever really get up and leave the room. I didn't mean it in the literal sense! Alternatively, you can do a couple of things which are more in line with my intention in telling you to "leave the room":

Mention, in a kind way (always kindness first), to those stakeholders (the "people seated at the table") that you see a lack of diversity.

If you decided you're done with a group, don't go yet! You can step out for a moment – let's call it a bathroom break – but make a private commitment to return to the meeting and bring with you people from those diverse backgrounds that we're speaking of. You know which ones you need here: the ones that don't look, act or think like your fellow table occupants – or sometimes, look, act or think even, like you.

With these invited perspectives, what new ideas can you generate?

It doesn't help anything if you just keep leaving. Here you have an opportunity to change the status quo. You can even set a new status quo.

We can be so afraid of diversity - but true diversity is only increasing, all over the world. I'm not just talking about race and gender. Of course, being a person with a disability, I'm used to considering diverse spectrums ranges of ability/disability, whether physical, or intellectual. When I talk about diversity, disability is a part of that, but I'm also talking about fundamental differences in everything from our upbringing to our values. In short, everything that makes each one of us unique. Of course, we're more the same than different; but that part is a hard sell.

Focus on getting diverse groups to the table in the first place and see what great things will happen from there. The world has many diverse and complex problems that can only possibly be solved by a diverse and complex mix of people.

EXERCISE

So, what can you do to ensure that as many people as possible who aren't currently present at the table get invited to have a seat?

____

____

____

____

____

____

____

____

If you have been the one that resisted opportunities for change and/or diversity in the past, list some reasons why:

____

____

____

____

____

____

____

____

How *could* you make it happen? Note: try to list the steps with the idea in mind that you have nothing to worry about. Really, this list is a private growth exercise for you that nobody else need ever see. Imagine the ideal scenario between you and this person/group of people. (Remember, you can't make *them* change at all.)

Now, how *will* you make it happen? Out of the list above, what's really doable for you?

What might be some negative comments you may hear as you take this opportunity to shake up the status quo? *(If you can anticipate, you can mitigate!)*

How might you respond to any negativity and disapproval you receive? (*Spoiler alert: there will probably be at least some.*)

Name three people you see in your daily life that could benefit from being invited to a particular "table" to join the conversation.

1.

2.

3. ____
____

What do you see in them?

1. ____
____

2. ____
____

3. ____
____

What sort of benefit do you think they would get from such an invitation?

1. ____
____

2. ____
____

3. ____
____

How will you invite them?

1. ____

____

2. ____

____

3. ____

____

Finally, examine your own motivation? (E.g. to step outside your comfort zone; to give someone an opportunity that might not otherwise receive it; to tap a person or group of people from outside your regularly frequented circles).

____

____

____

____

____

____

____

____

____

____

List more reasons behind your motivations:

____

____

____

____

____

CHEERS!

CONGRATULATIONS ARE IN ORDER. WE'VE discussed a lot here and now your journey continues. Hopefully as you move about your world having read this little book, there'll be a new sense of awareness, perhaps even a sense of urgency. Now, after reading, you can have a more critical observation of yourself and others. Your lens is freshly cleaned now, opened as wide as the aperture permits, facing outward and forward ready to capture all there is to see.

Remember to take time to reflect privately, as you have been practicing in these pages. Consider your own intentions with care, examining the internal thought-experiences that frame your views and motivations.

Move forward with intention, clear purpose and the right support structures in place. Along the way, gather those who are completely unlike you to join in.

Enjoy the journey and seek to gain as much from this one life to live as you possibly can.

The world awaits your awesome contributions.

Dear Reader,

For me, these stories are just the beginning. I have so many more lessons I need to and hope to learn, and once I've learned them I desire to share them with you. If nothing else, I pray that here in these pages you've found inspiration and encouragement, prompting you to think more objectively and critically about your every triumph and every obstacle. Now, go make good use of every experience and new revelation that God gives you. They are put in your path for a reason. Then, help someone else along the journey. Never, ever give up.

Words can't express how very happy I am to be able to share another kind of prose with you. While I still adore writing the romance novels that have been my main focus up to this point, I am delighted by this chance to offer you an encouraging word through real-life tales from my heart (and heartache). I hope these help you to reach your own brand of triumph.

Keep in touch with me, traveler! I anticipate publishing another collection of stories, this time with YOUR anecdotal advice for the road to travel. I'd be honored if you'd like to share.

If you were looking for my fiction, don't worry; more carefree, entertaining, and suspenseful escapes are on their way, soon.

I'd love to hear from you. Please visit me on line at **www.Teegarner.com** or if you are so inclined, write me a note at **teegarner@aol.com**. You can also write me a good-old fashioned letter. See the *About the Author* page for additional ways to contact me.

Here's to your journey and, until next time, may God richly bless you and keep you in His loving care.

Fondly,

Tracee

I carry the light in my pocket.
It shines even in the darkest hours.
I carry the light in my pocket;
I give handfuls of its power
to the weary and the heavy-burdened
who seek inspiration to empower.
They are the ones God asked us to inspire
with the lights in our pockets.
The light packers never tire,
because it is Thee
permitting us to be
the best light that others can see

~*TLG*

ABOUT THE AUTHOR

TRACEE LYDIA GARNER, A VIRGINIA native, is a bestselling and award-winning author. Her story *Family Affairs* won the BET First Time Writer's Contest, appearing in a story anthology titled "All That & Then Some". Tracee's other fiction titles include *Come What May*, *The One Who Holds My Heart, Love Unchosen and Anchored Hearts.* Tracee has also written poetry that won honorable mentions and has appeared in her alma mater's literary magazine. *Pack Light* is Tracee's first nonfiction book and she looks forward to many more volumes of anecdotal advice to share with you about her journey in this blessed life.

Tracee has a form of Muscular Dystrophy and uses a wheelchair. She is a full-time advocate for people with disabilities as a case manager for a health and human service organization in the DC area. In addition to her day job, Tracee teaches college-level writing courses and loves to read. She has a passion for assisting people and offering encouragement to expand their human potential.

Visit Tracee:
www.Teegarner.com
On Twitter **@Teegarner**
Like me on Facebook.com/**TraceeLydiaGarner**
On Instagram at **Teegarner**
On Pinterest at **Pinterest/Teegarner**

Write Tracee:

Tracee Lydia Garner
150 S. Sterling Blvd.
Suite 1106
Sterling,VA 20167

NOTES / REFLECTIONS

Made in the USA
Columbia, SC
21 September 2018